A Berlin Entrainment

Also by Peter Hughes

The Interior Designer's Late Morning, Many Press 1983
Bar Magenta (with Simon Marsh), Many Press, 1986
Odes on St. Cecilia's Day, Poetical Histories, 1990
The Metro Poems, Many Press, 1992
Psyche in the Gargano, Equipage, 1995
Paul Klee's Diary, Equipage, 1995
Keith Tippet Plays Tonight, Maquette Press, 1999
Blueroads: Selected Poems, Salt Publishing, 2003
Sound Signals Advising of Presence, infernal methods, 2006
Minor Yours, Oystercatcher Press, 2006
Nistanimera, Shearsman Books, 2007
The Sardine Tree, Oystercatcher, 2008
The Summer of Agios Dimitrios, Shearsman Books, 2009
Behoven, Oystercatcher, 2009
The Pistol Tree Poems (with Simon Marsh), Shearsman Books, 2011
Interscriptions (with John Hall), Knives Forks And Spoons Press, 2011
Regulation Cascade, Oystercatcher, 2012
Soft Rush, Red Ceilings Press, 2013
Quite Frankly, Like This Press, 2013
Selected Poems, Shearsman Books, 2013
Allotment Architecture, Reality Street, 2013
Quite Frankly (after Petrarch's Sonnets), Reality Street, 2015
Cavalcanty, Carcanet, 2017
via Leopardi 21, Equipage, 2017

Peter Hughes

A
Berlin
Entrainment

Shearsman Books

First published in the United Kingdom in 2019 by
Shearsman Books
50 Westons Hill Drive
Emersons Green
BRISTOL
BS16 7DF

Shearsman Books Ltd Registered Office
30–31 St. James Place, Mangotsfield, Bristol BS16 9JB
(this address not for correspondence)

www.shearsman.com

ISBN 978-1-84861-667-7

Acknowledgements
Some of these poems have previously appeared in:
*Blackbox Manifold, Crossways, Cumulus, Erotoplasty,
Golden Handcuffs Review, Leg Avant, Litter, The Lonely Crowd,
Molly Bloom, PN Review, Tears in the Fence* and *Tentacular.*

Contents

Ramblin'

a bunch of pink & nosy roses
climbs in through the bedroom window
looks around in late May breeze &
wonders where you are while Jack
O' Metty the excessively leggy lemon geranium
falls out of the bathroom window whenever
I open it to song courtesy of this fabulously
normal blackbird on the aerial opposite
& way above the place we put the bins
the day after we're supposed to & somewhere
you are wearing clothes & talking
to the neighbours as the Brad Mehldau Trio
sways its way around a bend of its own making
before mooching along Eden Street Backway
the days go by for the survivors & you
are now reclining in a European garden
relishing asparagus & Grüner Veltliner
well it's nice to take the weight off your head
shoulders knees & toes to reflect
upon another complex spa experience
& all those layered shadows in the forests
dank & spongy airmax footfalls
hush: all ECM & siskin   nibbling seasoned timber
nameless seeds & dented nuts & sampling woody herbs
& as I water ravaged salad
I have the thought: why don't we whistle too
you know just whistle whistle
everybody whistle back

Auguri

for Denise Riley, on her birthday

was it Ewan's lipstick
in the corner of the dark
blue pamphlet in my heart
well that'll do the trick
the direct line
along the spine to
London & then north
to Cambridge or the lane
past UEA to Yorkshire
then the longer prospects of all
the pictures you know the ones
in other people's houses or
wherever the galleries store
the current unselected staffed
by those who find it hard to park
& switch off the car radio
echoes with our passions
& we step back out
on wooden steps
that lead up to a cloudless sky
the top one loose

The Aselline Starlets

1

I said this imagery
was mental but
she claimed you
can't say what is
happening within
a composition
as the flicks & swerves
are too precise &
fast to verbalize
& also donkeys
are usually top heavy
as well as too
massive to catch when
suspended from your
thoughts & old arcs
carry memories
of awkward turns
& ecstasy
each thought is made
of temporary nodes
we sometimes fresco
on the ceiling
but usually do not
because you know
death intervenes
or we get banished
from our provinces
by the council or the
gravities of love
& cooking then learning
this new scale or
trying to catch a flatfish

or anticipating flight
again become
the medium in which
these things happen
but we nearly know
it's impossible except in
certain kinds of art
to fly forever

2

we try to fly
above the heads
of propaganda
we partner novel forces
& the fatal graphs
of lost momentum
the show's constructed
on a person's wrist
sweaty & chaffing
lost in lights
made up
accommodating
glitter falling
balancing above
a couple of tunes

3

all the goodness
sucked out of the
neighbours & bound
to a stick with

mallarky & duct tape
was what they opted
to salute & strive for
songs of old rope
& sail-cloth embellished
with the sooty mould
of who gives a shit
we proceeded to erect
this monument to
the history of art
about camping & sex
with crumbs & mildew
where the nearest
place for milk was Wales
it's as if you go back
to an old town that's
dead in you forever
each time you open
your mouth to speak
& no speech comes

4

we dreamt there'd
been a rupture
in the weather
& we were entering
Steve Swallow's
disco period sideways
late into the night
I read the tattoo'd lady
without really
taking it in
the waste-ground
wind is whispering

we each have
decomposing caravans
parked inside our heads
rats' droppings
sketches &
rubber jewels
wait for the moon
to make the first move

5

no-one came from
miles around these fields
of moonlit pumpkin
the substitute ring-
meister can't decide
whether to dance in
bed to Chopin or lean
out of the flap to see
if it's the bailiffs
one of the flying goats
is off on an away day
to express this
play any note
well not that one
a semitone higher
or lower
& nod

6

I'm no longer
with the circus

except sometimes
briefly in the memory
of strangers
I reached a point
where all I saw
were messages
from Mary
cross-stitched on
those overarching
canvas skies
still I do do the same
route at the same times
sleep in the car
register the music
now & then
with the window down
when the wind is right
but we don't interact
the time for such things
closed its eyes & rolled
back under the waves
they never see me park
or circle the compound
or swoop overhead

Map

it's hard to start
new notebooks
so I usually fill
the first few pages
with my new addresses
& the name of the local
bar & station
which is Sonnenallee
quotes are also good
while the sun on the floor
of the library
creeps all the way up
to my shoes
I should've brought water
as well as a pen
the city's full
of verdant spaces
but by the time I leave
they're turning grey
& changing demographic
all the dirty lights come on
& sing through the heart
breaking fragrances of hot vegetable oil
night walks
across the squares
& pages & a map
of the last town
I found in my back pocket
crossed with worn out creases
that open into gaps

Lift

for Jennifer Wiseman

I

*

night buds
listening to whispers
of the past
& present
darkness sensing
a dismantling
of the garden
colder waters
insinuate
themselves
under every door
listening in
to whispers
of the past & present
darkness palpable
starts of intuition
which one
night come to consciousness
of other wings
& flights
& listen
to the whispers
stars are blossoming
thoughts of their appearance
harmonising what is
left of time

*   *

2

for weeks
we remembered
to water
the plastic tub
of salad plants
I lift it up
to give it
to a neighbour
as we leave
& am caught off guard
& startled
by its lightness

*

(Dr Jennifer Wiseman works for NASA as an astrophysicist, and is the senior project scientist for the Hubble Space Telescope. We overlapped as visiting Fellows at Magdalene College, Cambridge).

Poem at the Equinox

I've started swinging tins on string around my head
to try to talk to some of what still squats
the boarded up accommodation of the sky
crackling & pulling
especially in afternoons of thunder
when what comes next darts past dressed up in night &
        kitchen light
feels like a cheap betrayal of two or three imaginary friends
the wet dog English dusk hits mud
but now you've got it up
& swinging you can hear the ocean
or maybe the soup & all the pressure making crimson lines
with white surrounds across the hands & seas
to company that shows no sign of coming
to an understanding of funding or independence
or distinctions between centrifugal force & hormones
& here's to a host of absent friends
who have all moved on through currency
fluctuations & access courses or class cleansing
one could do worse than be a swinger of tins
you don't have to listen to soup or wind resistance
turned out they'd just been once around the block
we had a conversation on the nature of attachments
we could listen to each other or shorten the line
we could change our names & just play modern conkers
I dented some old constellations
& left a few abrasions on my shins
& I is just a section of the gaps between the doors
& frames which get a little looser every winter
tie tin to string with granny knots
or pop it in the orange net the onions came in
stick your finger in the sky to check that it's still there
watch out for frisbees & apparent UFOs
watch out for crop-circle spotters

watch out for the uniformed helicopters
watch out for the police who help us all breathe
we're swinging tins of soup around our heads
mine is made of squash & bits of bacon
it's really an unfunded installation
it's also an affordable weapon
it's basically a satellite of love

Plenum

for Patricia Farrell

& so you danced
in these new spaces
drawn & then transformed
by thought through vistas
ruled & etched
rotated swerves
inhabited considered
how it's never how
it all looks back at us
shimmering & stirred
by your attentions
the gratifying surfaces
hovers in heat haze
registers horizons
as they take a few
steps back & bow

The Spirit of Cricket

she whispered hi I bring you tidal flats
& a sky turned inside out & heaving
with tricksy species of bacteria
those wind-borne vacillating presences
responsible for memory loss & swing
halfway though the third test we found ourselves
besieged by length & diminishing light
caught on the crease & handcuffed by nightmares
in which we all wore orange & were marched
in pairs forever through the members' room
& the corridors of uncertainty
to that patch of thistle dock & dogs' muck
where we first learned how to bowl the wrong length
& how to snick bald tennis balls to slip

After Bach

return to where
& when the spring
still spirals upwards
from an absence
in the ground
a rope of water
swaying downwards
to a darkness
from the winter
sky where light
breaks over ice
& old doors
open as supplies
arrive for meals
& memory &
this furniture
is pushed right back
against the walls
in preparation
for the dance
the shortest day
is coming
to an end
the music sings
beyond the fields
& here & now
the water
fills again
with stars

Hard Yards

for Isabel, Sid & Ivy

parked on your left
in the Commercial Tavern
this evening we're essentially
dogs with soft tops & damp soft
toys & chandeliers gleaming
lugubriously above the aroma
of Tottenham Beavertown
Brewery's finest concoctions
we dumped our bags in some hotel
& rode that Ramsgate train
but not for long what with this
being our stop & Chuck Berry
throwing in the brothel creepers
guitar pick & hi-end surveillance
installations after the second pint I think
I hear out of this Woody Allen film
do not desire to go but they've got
hot gnocchi & Ivy getting on for
16 months is putting in the hard yards
around the thrilling tables
up the fascinating stairs
after voyaging to Whitechapel & Cassiopeia
with all the dangling mobile phones
& now the kid's bike in a glass case
which reminds us of the days before
he stumped up the deposit on a shark
we pedalled into bushes in the dark
we breathed too fast & pushed ourselves
off the ends of all the built-in shelves
into a weirdly backlit vision of the future
with the doors blowing open on their own
as the London evening strolls back in
& takes its place with us around this table

Stir Fry

as you stir
the next component
of the stir fry
& rest your foot
against your knee
in the position
of the heron
or is it called the frog
I conclude
my own offensive
on the onion
& I wonder
how we managed
to end up
here & now
still in one piece

On Leaving Cork

the recording
informs us
we're reversing
past a guy in
yellow weeding
plastic flowers
outside the city hall
a bar pulls up
beside myself
announcing WINE
BEER COCKTAILS
& though I've never
had a wine beer
cocktail there's a
momentary pang
as the bus eases
forwards from one
missed opportunity
to who knows where
I try to read but can't
stop imagining you
naked on a white
summer coverlet
I move uneasily & change
my seat to get a better
view of summer trees
along the road & your
astonishing reflection
in all these ways
my throat goes
dry I'm heading back
towards you now with plans
for a new cocktail
called Momentary Pang

clink cheers & *alla nostra*
drain the loaded glasses
place them down
upon this bedside table

Talking Windows

atmospheric traffic
nudges an old window
then the other
on the far side of the room
responds with rumbling shudders
the windows talk
about the keeper of the bees
they talk about the here & now
they talk about the holder of the queen
the windows talk
of moths & moons
desire & ruptured sashes
they want me to open the curtains
in order to be filled
with your reflections
as you flit
towards the bathroom
in nothing but my T-shirt
& the snow begins in darkness
the windows & the world ascend through silence
as the snow goes on
you may come back

Heading off the Poussin at the Pass

for Gareth Prior

if your urine is the shade
of north Roman straw & balances bouquets
of slowly roasted artichokes
it may be time to stop regarding it
with quite so much attention
yes even if it glints with mercurial
reflections redolent of Ponte Rotto
& all the demands of Roman elevenses
programmatic light orchestral suites & ah
digestive tracts of unweened lambs
alongside unexamined flute parts
see how the subdued light is sneaking in
from the top left to illuminate the end
of the bed & the daughter's rude health
a doctor rubs some extra virgin
oil on the eyelids of the lapsed protagonist
they carry out a little jug of liquid —
goodbye father — on the wall an empty
circle faces us with a couple of doors
into oblivion or the dining room
the last track on the album has finished
it's been on mute the whole time

A Beer for Ulf

voices of the villages & specialists
who can distinguish between porridge
& let's say insulation foam are now
regarded with suspicion by those managers
who keep appealing to the readers' shifty
sense of vulnerability when looking at this
new world we've all inhabited for years

the big rhymes become impatient
with all the little noises in between
& vowels change shape to blend in
or stand out & flicker in the sky
& higher tides & the luminous presence
between the words & bottles on the far side
of the room we ask ourselves again

which nouns are proper as the fire & night
outside the windows whisper with
their own supply of noises yet to be
deciphered or erased or mistranslated
three of which have not been heard before
we have time to analyse the sounds
behind the noises rumours & *geräusche*

a large one falls out of a tree
there where the grass was cut
this afternoon & brazen leaves
were shredded into artificial recipes
autobiographies & misprisions so
much better than the real ones
could ever begin to be negotiated

they even featured the trumpet
of an angel playing silently as

English & German met in Rome
or Cambridge & enjoyed a passeggiata
before or after dinner it's important
to try to make sense & contact & fail
with grace a little further down the road

on the western side of the valley
the land rises to an almost
vertical escarpment where more
resistant rocks caress the sky
& pretend to understand
each other & forget about the radical
components not to mention the angels

in the work of centuries ago
they used as duvets & fabric
for adverts but why would you
vote against the planet that supports you
as if it were a reactionary parent
good for nothing & holding you back
from your shiniest manifestation

well we're just going to live inside
our heads they said except for gala
openings to which we'll be escorted
in massive air-conditioned vehicles
with proper nouns & fingers in our ears
to keep out sounds that never rhyme
with our names & titles chiselled

in the skulls of drains on our resources
seize the day & wrench it backwards
build a tower on higher ground far
inland & ring-fenced against everything
including history & humanity & Ulf
steps to the left & his halo disappears
to be replaced by these our stunned night skies

Old Rope

we lean into the wind
a little traffic noise
the first half-sensed exemplary stars

holm oak   hibiscus
the rope   & lavender

a tuff substratum

a few more
unfamiliar voices
through the shutters

someone stuffing gold back underground

Song-Song

a longish introduction to the waltz
displays pulsating yearning
in the bass & gives us time
to walk around the instrument
or pop back through the wings
for one more segment of scotch egg /
contemporary beverage
    inhale a palate-cleansing
    onshore breeze of parazone
perhaps segment is the wrong word
        wenn du bei mir bist
    I think about your birthday
        most days actually
as well as the dynamics of the duo
or the trio if you count the poem
which has this way of keeping
time whilst moving on to welcome
back two stars now reappearing
between the much-loved blackbird tree
& the largely-ignored telegraph pole
anyway eventually the piano
wanders in at about
the same time
as we start touching
& exchanging
all these keys

In the art

in the art
the weather starts
to change where we are walking
on delicate translucent steps
& golden trellises
hover in the troposphere
with neighbours from Byzantium
& branches turning into amber
just outside our bodies
outside in the sense
of in & all around the wires
enable you to turn
turn in to your own astronaut
out on an away day
indulging in a space walk
on the surface of the earth
knee deep in data
then up to & over the ears
connected to a life line
the inner unborn child
soon to relinquish
& locate its key connections
time to play a solo on
the last string of one's
own marionette
this mirror image
this imaginary robot
approaches a new crisis
of discovery
the forks & crossroads
& accumulated choices
never made or taken
or translated & arrayed
as glistening code

& beached upon the island of
the self we start to find new
views & unfamiliar footprints
an island
as the man said
full of strange noises
& unexpected weather
the awesome & fictitious
company we'd forgotten
we had been
the knight
what does he do
& why are we still here
in an origami landscape that unfolds
into transforming novel spaces
strung out forever
in the humming
space between
expectation & fulfilment

(This poem was written in response to Fred Baker's amazing
virtual reality project through which one can walk into a Klimt).

Hike

here she comes
the fallen leaves
get back up

Life Writing: in memoriam John James

the proliferation of Cambridge street food stalls
shows no sign of slowing down John
& I'm sitting eating in the market place
while a guy plays the guitar
in front of the monument to Snowy
me with a fistful of Mediterranean sausage
nestling in a bright refreshment of mixed salad
invigorated by a generous ejaculation of chilli sauce
as your man moves on
to a song about feeling it in your fingers
& feeling it in your toes
though I am mainly feeling it in the pit
I neglected to mention the cucumber
& mint tinged yoghurt lining
the whole dense wrap where the sausage is halal
& the music here is free
& finds its way into the witnesses & sky
we cock an eye at now & blink
away an inappropriate sad anger
reflecting on the Irish referendum
Windrush & the grotesque stupidities of Brexit
we join in with barely audible humming
bodily registration of the rhythms
a tapping foot or two fingers patting the thigh
the sun is moving round the building
& in the circumstances John
I'm going to fuck shamelessly
with the playlist & he effortlessly
segues into a moving instrumental
take on love is the drug

A
Berlin
Entrainment

S-BAHN-RING BERLIN

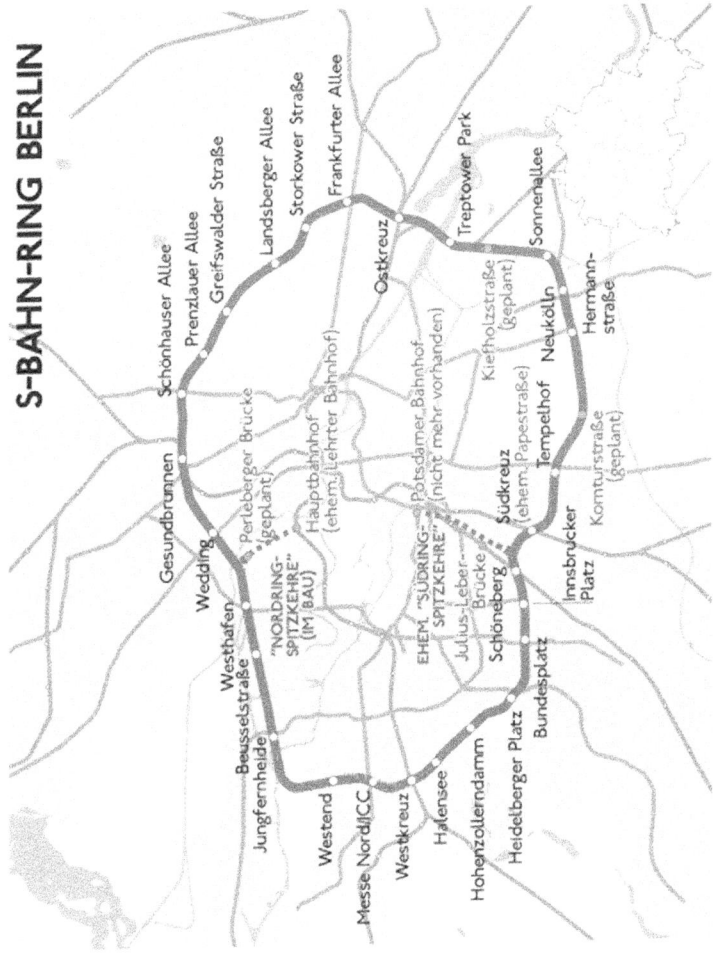

Schönhauser Allee
Prenzlauer Allee
Greifswalder Straße
Landsberger Allee
Storkower Straße
Frankfurter Allee

Treptower Park
Sonnenallee

Ostkreuz

Kiefholzstraße (geplant)
Neukölln
Hermann-straße

Gesundbrunnen
Wedding
Westhafen

Perleberger Brücke (geplant)
"NORDRING-SPITZKEHRE" (IM BAU)

Hauptbahnhof (ehem. Lehrter Bahnhof)

Potsdamer Bahnhof (nicht mehr vorhanden)

EHEM. "SÜDRING-SPITZKEHRE"
Julius-Leber-Brücke

Südkreuz (ehem. Papestraße)

Tempelhof

Komturstraße (geplant)

Innsbrucker Platz

Beusselstraße
Jungfernheide

Westend
Messe Nord/ICC
Westkreuz
Halensee
Hohenzollerndamm
Heidelberger Platz
Bundesplatz

Schöneberg

Gesundbrunnen

so what was being
translated into
the lethargic English

of the last few years
yellowing under carpet
or boxed up in the attic

of a house long since
demolished in what passes
for & through my mind

Some of the wells are dried up springs, the water table dropping as we speak, then falling even more when we have spoken. Take what you need and be my guest. The remains of the world caught on certain temporary thorns and then dismembered by the wind. Two woman tinker with an amp and a receiver, the casings made of low-background steel. The salad tastes of cinders and wrecked atmospherics.

Schönhauser Allee

the next illuminated island
metal sheds in the heavens
trains going over our heads in the dark

talk of etymology
saunter through the afternoons
& evenings that remain

where autumn smells of Trakl
Keats & Rilke when you prise
the lid off an old tin of treacle

The traffic overhead gets louder, here in the oily concrete
pit of a service bay that closed down twenty years ago.
Crashes in the atmosphere. Spare parts from the 1930s still
stacked on metal shelves. Beautiful adverts for lubricants
framed in quiet rust. Exhausted pipes on racks.

Prenzlauer Allee

the warm bar eventually closes
outside crystals of ideas of frost
consolidate one upon the other

a flower pot of cigarette ends
a lost finger-puppet fox in the night
she turns aside into her hair & strides

over chilling parallel lines
a pickle-fork sgraffito in the table
glittering tram tracks into distance

Scraps of text folded into new and labile combinations through which we peer out at strangely unfamiliar spaces, scarcely bearable, full of promise. Authorities implement the wishes of those who wouldn't be seen dead in this zone. Slash the budget for the dumbfounded, facilitate choice tax cuts. A Sunday morning years ago not quite going to plan. The very notion of a plan gradually softened, dried out and then dropped off. The waves still strike the shore. The washing still gets done. The sky is slowly darkening, developing a brassy and unwholesome sheen.

Greifswalder Straße

well before dawn
mumbling Klee puppets
perched in a dead trilingual tree

in this acidic half-light
gradually brightening
to reveal as from an ache

a distressed green chair
by an empty desk
a door leading into a new visibility

The sun rises with reluctance as the Earth turns over restlessly and all the bad ideas blink and settle in uncountable rooms in this new morning light. New crowds beached inside themselves after a storm, the ships now sunk. The tendency to recall and dwell upon those childhood TV programmes in which bits of household waste were reassembled to make inexpensive, useless gifts. Sit in the chair of a stranger.

Landsberger Allee

pedal down the boulevard
playing truth or dare with dodgy
invites or contemporary lyrics

white-van lads who kill
mosquitoes with the sun
she accompanies this Cecil Taylor tune

it's still switched on
the artist on the kerb blows over
the mouth of an empty bottle

The music involves contradictions and cannot take shape in a soundproof room. There are usually a few shared base notes, according to the training course. The Earth turning, a blend of food processors and that guy blowing over the mouth of a bottle, sobbing from upstairs and shouting in the next street. The hush of a passing limousine sounds like nerve gas and a new security procedure. The skies slide shut again.

Storkower Straße

exact red berries reflecting on
cold water / vibrations
a final sip now try to sleep install

a blue translucent skylight in the roof
of your own mouth & meditate upon
scuffs & cracks

lose lightness keep sleeplessness
company check time
& trip over consonants in the dark

Feral shrubs and weeds, madonnas and orphans of the sidings, the constant promise of a new world on the right or wrong side of the tracks. The promise of a new idea, a proper sleep, some comfortable boots in which to leave the station, head towards the centre, collect the child. The cold absences of town are where the homeless try to sleep. Rosehips, haws and pomegranate seeds.

Frankfurter Allee

no light left except the glow
the city makes while car doors close
laughter leaves the bars

fear & celebration
a canny team sows toxic seeds
into a scarcity of air

the bass accompaniment keeps shifting
from block to block & head to head the dead
musicians play on long into the night

Goodwill and companionship are strangled by dense strands of interwoven lying on the airwaves, malice and misinformation laced with disingenuous greed. In unfurnished back rooms, and bleak cellars, or at the top of the stairs in these old back street blocks, a few new songs are brought to birth and nurtured. The availability and cost of child care still transforms our lives and art. The uninformed know precisely who to blame. Our reflections pick up speed again and merge.

Ostkreuz

shopping for fleas
in the lee of Sauron's
pied-à-terre

pick up a tinny ring
distressed green chair
& worn out plate

we turn into the husks
of our beginnings
quietly rattling

Work around the station never stops. Desire lines are confirmed, enhanced by new generations of weeds on either side. We forget where the old paths went. This is where we go these days. These are now the outlines of our lives. The air sags with dust and diesel fumes. A wave of sunlight or a new idea still breaks upon the city. There is already everything we need, but fatally arranged.

Treptower Park

narrow-gauge rails swerve into the mouth
of a plastic beast & now seem less alluring
the years go by held down by rusted nuts

& fog-bound sympathetic resonance
as if you could carve out a cylinder
of sky & wrap it as a solstice gift

all our strangers start out again each day
with less support & a watery lunch
with no baggage they feel light on their feet

Empty barrels with ragged labels patted up the ramp into the light. No need to ask whose voice this is. A woman with big gloves by her side squats against the lorry and rolls another cigarette. She thinks about her grandad who died a year ago and her mum who died last week. A gaggle of young men pass by & spit remarks into her lap. They raise their mouths and laugh at the sky. Sudden sunlight floods the platform. You feel the next train coming.

Sonnenallee

a suntanned man & woman
rummage through the rubbish for the empties
as morning breaks again across the station

a ruptured purse discarded on the tracks
with broken glass & half-arsed terza rima
voices of the city pick up speed

heaven bound & choked to death on diesel
our impact trails return to haunt our dreams
where love & hunger pulse & realign

Hard to remember where we first heard this music, where and when we started out. The fascination of what's left along the tracks and what will be revealed tomorrow morning. Dreams of the CERN particle accelerator, the rustle of the data from a series of collisions. It's how they're finding out about the world. That, and sniffing. Belated entrainment, we stagger in the slipstream. Cut to a peak, panning vertigo, erasure, annihilation. Sit still being swept along past past, past present, past fireflies synching their displays and getting eaten.

Neukölln

the city writes itself into the bones
eyes & other containers
a fleck of grit for every shell

washed up in the precincts of the Rixdorf
a name to save in case we get a dog
to promenade along Karl-Marx-Straße

into the courtyard of the Café Rix
with its green furniture & promises
a cold bowl of water under the table

I don't know what they squirt behind their ears here but it misses and merges with the heaps of burnt-out fireworks, the gauzy fast-food aftermaths, the latest negotiations. In certain atmospheric conditions, and if the chemicals align, an aurora borealis of failure stretches across the sky like an advert for yoga while litter and the latest catch words end up stuck in shrubs around the supermarket carpark. We'll stay friends. The dogs are pretty optimistic except for the ones thrown out on the street at the start of the summer holidays years ago. They still believe in God.

Hermannstraße

show me the way to the veg & pharmaceuticals
futures scored across the sky
above a junk shop stuffed with kitchen chairs

archaeological technologies
moles on acid excavate the darkness
scrimshaw punctuates solitary afternoons

sat on a bench by the kebab van
I see the girl in the repossessed shop
still staring at a single glowing pear

This is the flat, the home, and that's the kitchen window. The flat has been divided and is occupied by strangers once again. The fireworks were amazing. Not beautiful, but striking. I thought of empty tunnels running underneath the city. Is it best to pick up a syringe discarded by the bench and put it in a bin? Or is that more dangerous to whoever might come rummaging? Best to leave it in plain sight. Some projects fail. The enormous metal lampshade in the bedsit came from a skip outside a factory which has just closed down.

Tempelhof

the ways these overlapping leaves
jostle attentiveness around a light
hunger pouring over another lip

ride the ring around the rim with one voice
singing in a rediscovered language
heard towards the ending of a journey

to where they smoke a little lunchtime weed
& fly the taut & acrobatic kites
wings of desire unfurled & then let go

At dusk you see imagined outlines of proposed accommodation with figures moving across living room windows, flickering blue screens and memories of orange kites. Shimmering balconies in the sky with bikes and skateboards, herbs in pots, orange gas cylinders, a broken BBQ, a trumpet on a plastic table. They're just ideas. People's dreams meet up above the disused airport and smile, have a drink, compare notes. New hallucinations are gathering on the far side of the horizon. They don't come from elsewhere.

Südkreuz

we had the chance to leave the circle
of the dog-head & head for the sun
& yet we swing around towards the north

damaged hour & minute hands resisting
gravity to let us surf the dangers
of the sun our local dignitary

master the minute clicks of facial
recognition the next phase of a flight
past the city of dreams & the black hole

The rusty iron anchor in the head, part buried in clay &
guilt, alluvial deposits, fly-tipped junk from old addresses.
The weird figure on the is it called the bowsprit. Bows.
Bows? The inner mists and smears across the mirror.
They start queuing before dawn but few get as far as the
door before the office closes. The line goes right around
the block so the person at the front can be standing near
the last in line. They could all join hands and form a
ring around the buildings. In one of the shop windows,
a wide TV screen. High resolution. The colours artificial.
Kodachrome. It shows a speeded up film of the changing
seasons with an oak tree centre stage. Everyone walks by.

Schöneberg

we drifted back to work after futile
lunchtime meetings in Buddha's Muesli Bar
where Donald lost a trumpet in his beard

years ago along with over-ripened
aubergine extruded through the senseless
lattices of late Thursday afternoons

so much Veltliner down among the bones
we stumble down this rocking corridor
two notes crying through the base of the train

The guy at the bar is drunk, seething about the school shooting. It happened in the town where he was born, the town where his nephew and nieces still live, as far as he knows. He is slurring his speech about government spending, about the columns in some graph. Education, he shows a modest space between forefinger and thumb. Healthcare, he moves his finger two millimetres. The military, he rests his left hand in his lap, raises his right arm high in an aggressive gesture, overbalances and crashes from his stool onto the floor. He's sobbing, deep convulsions, several seconds between each heave, he bites his mouth until it bleeds.

Innsbrucker Platz

lines begin to merge the intercities
& the undergrounds the dozing off &
coming to in half-imaginary

neighbourhoods all rhythmic & hypnotic
sort of simmering to lunch & music
a rag and bone merchants' convention

the bent satellites cruise by observing
vacant reflections & the warm-blooded
travellers dreaming deep inside their phones

Hard to synchronise your habits to the rhythms of this town. The background noise throughout the hours of darkness makes little sense as you keep moving but it feels blue and vital. We're dancing with imaginary partners and the sales team is looking on, taking notes. See what parts of us to steal, rename and then sell back. In the daytime people recuperate in corners and relate to their toothbrushes on charge. Then the contest starts again to see who can be elsewhere in as many ways as possible while staying put. A forgotten drama layered over the next and so on. Company. Signs of life from all around the world are thickening the blood like wine.

Bundesplatz

a little swig of chilly Wein von Wien
& out into the vacillating streets
to check out all the apothecaries

Alcatraz & scary neon florists
then into another windswept station
where a canvas bag has been abandoned

he's says: I'm just another King's Cross fox
who can't stand coleslaw or blue celery
I want to have what he's had but too late

The ecology of the underground is changing as we see from these new growths. It's getting younger as the years go by; we're not sure how many there are left. A new student movement flows away from the old wrought iron gates. Less relish these days in listening to the latest killer track. We go around the ring again *tschilp tschilp* we're entering the bend and looking for a white line where we pass on the baguette and flute.

Heidelberger Platz

witnessing the storm of wings descending
through glimpses of the ghostly breadcrumb trails
that kink towards the entrance to the mine

the rim rings & echoes in our hollows
headlines scribbled on inflatable dolls
rise high into the air & drift away

we step around the weatherbeaten guy
skirt around the never to be written
& stalk towards perhaps an hour later

A costly musical based on a cartoon version of a fairy tale. Let's say a miniature princess with a haddock's tail who loses her voice, is trapped in a thorn bush and enjoys the hospitality of several tiny men for whom she cooks and cleans. A dragon made of lengths of 2x1 covered in the skins of big cats and flags, operated by people in black who can't be seen. Here comes the messenger with this evening's news which has again been generously provided by the palace. Turns out approval ratings for the palace are higher than ever so we are to have a big parade.

Hohenzollerndamm

they move to guard the borders of the air
we continue to pretend we hadn't heard
about the banishment of strangers

in these unexpected conversations
we find ourselves the last ones at the bar
then sit a little longer in the sky

outside we watch each other watching slow
encroachments of blue abstracted shadows
installations around the theme of home

The arms industry and gun lobby are feeling particularly patriotic and expansive this morning. They'd like to teach potential customers a thing or two. It's complicated. Watch out for infiltration. If any of your neighbours have ever done a kindness report it to the church or clan. We donated a bazooka to the janitor, don't mention it. To enhance safety. Dinner ladies keep a Glock behind each pot. Eat your greens junior.

Halensee

the other driver might be waving back
dusk remote in the glow of snow
three chimneys on the skyline

a bigger brother wreathed in navy cloud
by the station a lamppost winged with two
great lights is a weird apocalyptic

bat impaled on our forgotten oaths
go below the blue bridge who played on that
did I have the album & let it go

The blue tango and the blue tangle well we never did find that address. Crippled by wondering what would have happened if we had. Now I have room in my drawer. The trees continue to lose and find their leaves. Unfamiliar species are provisionally identified, gasping at low tide. Some die of their own weight in this strange setting. The first waves of the revolution will be filmed on phones, turned into an unrelated cartoon then made into a musical which features life-size puppets and a homemade dragon. It's already a set text.

Westkreuz

skinny helter-skelter on the skyline
bleak & disused maypole requisitioned
for dark arts what now inner squatter

awkward white gazebo departures
are acid we hear them burn through girders
& continental icepacks monitored

by stained bears with huge paws & the faces
of exhausted gods north ring & south ring
meet at Westkreuz where a sky is dying

Too late to counterfeit shares in a fine New Zealand
bunker plus hobbit handyman and gardener. Foreigners
wear horns. My unchanged way of life is what my father
fought for. My personal trainer is teaching me to breath
underwater. First the cinema shows us the way and then
the police take up the baton. The whole place is now
a recreational facility for those who worked so hard to
inherit. You can pay to sit next to me in Burger King.

Messe Nord/ICC

soothing summer rain that orchestrates these
visionary skies between the branches
out over slaughter lake we make our way

back to the train & scratchy headphone sounds
someone else's rap or unsuccessful
language course or what might be another

Beirut come-back track the little Turkish
girl in an azure dress is teaching both
her stroppy younger brothers how to count

We thought we glimpsed the Eiffel Tower, the bus route underwater, components of other walls made out of crushed, recycled language. You invited us into your garden, then locked gates and unleashed dogs. Now you bulldozer the ancestors' gardens and build rest rooms over their bones. This is the only place to learn another language but the necessary language hasn't yet been written, the mother tongue.

Westend

the big pink cuboid by the rails
near the country track with someone's trumpet
playing on a balcony alongside

two bicycles & seven wheels with time
to register the beauty of the curves
along the lines that travel round the head

passengers for Tegel airport change here
but stay on for another chorus
the line-up will never be repeated

Every other weekend that tricksy double dip as you cross over the tracks; relative and conditional. The constellations slowly change but the puddle at the crossroads stays the same. Compaction. Compaction still has a lot to answer for but remains unable to speak. Everybody's life feels abstract this evening, the streetlight catching random spatters. And yet the purple light of hunger is a dark claw reaching upwards from the gut to rearrange the world, talk about the props and lighting.

Jungfernheide

we came from different places & stayed there/
here despite the years of separation
warped concentric rings reciprocating

filters for a few views of foliage
the awe-inspiring weight of two tomb stones
balanced on straws a birch among

the sycamores punctuated by the
one lop-sided nest perched in the top-left
branch a magpie's or a cancellation

The girdle of emotional support can be restrictive; you feel exceedingly vertical as if confronting these nocturnal elements in artificial lunar light, a Hepworth piece left standing in the unemployed north Cornish hail. That can't be right. The intolerable grinding, the food mixer remains switched on however much is in the actual bowl. I could have been a delicately poised substantive in an elegant yet sensitively nuanced late syntactic dark negotiation but that is to misunderstand how language and the human subject... wait: this is but prose.

Beusselstraße

Florian & Jeremy get married
the cuisine is Viennese the city
in the sunset decides to turn light green

revivified the band begins to play
intangible cultural heritage
an edgy contemporary tango

where we take it in turns to be leading
wiry flamenco now dimming the lights
we dance at the edge of the loading bays

When she first came here she spent days on end without speaking to a soul. Then she taught herself guitar. What is this now? A feeling that visits the outside of your mouth but then flutters away towards an opening. Towards the window, an artificial light source or the time you can't forget or quite remember when the moth touched your lip and then lapsed back towards the flame. Someone holds a cold glass up into a cloudless sky and stares right through it. She taught herself guitar so she could hear her own voice singing.

Westhafen

the sky behind the cranes & frogs in ponds
eviscerated warehouses where else
could we have met now that they're bringing down

the startled trees & their inhabitants
drains clogged up with fertile mulch & chunky
vegetation funk struggling to survive

the languid wavelengths of this hipster bar
Lager Hell & far too much vibrato
in the glasses leaves nervous surfaces

Fashions change and sometimes trees and people get in the way, especially in Sheffield or the Amazon, where loggers have no time to pee, and fewer trees to pee against or under. The future's bright and wears a vivid halo. Unwholesome is the next decade's top word and apocalyptic high-tides evict the marginal. Move on up amidst the ravaged and regrettable. Radioactive nails scrape and delve.

Wedding

from the bar's haven it's just a cat's jump
to this leaden thrill of sickness shouting
up the *Musikantenknochen* to the

brain as another shaman makes her way
along the spirit vines to echoes of
dead musicians harmonising with wheels

& blowing up a storm called Ringbahn tour
in which we dream the tallest trees come down
to leave a space for these new worlds to grow

The world aches and the healers are reviled. These costly courses in synchronised jeering are becoming more extreme. So much evidence exists to show you punched yourself and you deserved it. Like the finer rootlets of trees the more productive networks have been meeting in the dark. They share minerals and hunches. They kiss after hours. Acres of social deprivation crack open into new configurations. Cleaners of the fields and airwaves are trying to agree upon a nominated driver.

www.ingramcontent.com/pod-product-compliance
Lightning Source LLC
Chambersburg PA
CBHW020213090426
42734CB00008B/1050